Keepers of
What Matters Most

Other titles by Emily Freeman

Keepers of
What Matters Most

A Young Woman's Guide
to Living the Values

Emily Freeman

DESERET
BOOK

Salt Lake City, Utah

For Megan, Grace, Maggie, Annie, Katie, Brooklin,
Savvy, Ella, Kemry, Kaylen, Maddie, and Abby
Never forget how truly important, precious, and valuable you are

Text © 2010 Emily Belle Freeman

Library of Congress Cataloging-in-Publication Data
Freeman, Emily, 1969–
  Keepers of what matters most : a Young Woman's guide to living the values / Emily Freeman.
     p. cm.
  Includes bibliographical references.
  ISBN 978-1-60641-234-3 (paperbound)
  1. Young women—Religious life. 2. Young women—Conduct of life. 3. Young Women (Church of Jesus Christ of Latter-day Saints) I. Title.
  BX8643.Y6F74 2010
  248.8'43—dc22   2009042217

Printed in China

R.R. Donnelley, Shenzhen, China
10   9   8   7   6   5   4   3   2   1

A note from the author

Recently I had the opportunity to spend an evening with Ardeth Kapp, the General Young Women's President who introduced an entire generation of girls to seven values that would forever change their lives for good. As I asked her about those values, her eyes lit up, and her excitement bubbled over just as it had on October 18, 1987, when she first introduced the Young Women theme.

During our conversation, Sister Kapp explained that her presidency's greatest hope was to help each young woman discover her true identity. The theme became an answer to four heartfelt questions. *Who am I?* A daughter of our Heavenly Father. *What am I to do?* Stand as His witness. *How will I do it?* Live the young women values. *Why?* So that I will be prepared to make and keep sacred covenants, receive the ordinances of the temple, and enjoy the blessings of exaltation.

Just like you, I grew up repeating the theme every Sunday in Young Women's. I came to believe I was a daughter of our Heavenly Father who loves me. I wanted to stand as His witness. I learned to love the values as I lived them. They led me to the temple.

I express deepest gratitude to Ardeth Kapp and her presidency for sharing these values with the world. They have had a profound influence on my life.

Many years ago there was a remarkable celebration that took place at sunrise on October 11, 1986, when 300,000 balloons containing messages of hope were released around the world. As you finish this book, perhaps you could have a celebration of your own, sharing your message with the world, as you become a keeper of what matters most.

There are all different kinds of keepers. Some girls are scorekeepers and others are goal-keepers. Perhaps you are a secret keeper, or maybe you are a journal keeper. I wonder if you have ever heard of a light keeper?

Are you a keeper?

The responsibilities of a keeper can include looking after something or protecting something fragile or valuable. That makes sense. A goalkeeper at a soccer game would have to protect the goal, and a light keeper is someone who looks after a lighthouse to make sure the light is always lit. A keeper, then, could be thought of as someone who protects, guards, or looks after something that is important, precious, or valuable.

My grandmother was the keeper of a trunk that is filled with magical memories. Did you ever play dress-up? If so, you would love looking through my Grandma Belle's trunk. Sometimes when we would go for an afternoon visit we would beg my grandmother to pull out the old trunk. Then we would carefully lift each item from the trunk as Grandma Belle told us the stories that filled her life.

The trunk has several different compartments inside. In one compartment there is an old forty-five-star American flag that hung from the upstairs balcony of my grandma's home, and in another, a crazy quilt handstitched in 1912, with all different colors of triangles and squares. Some of the compartments contain old high-button shoes and the special tools to hook each button through the hole, and some have antique purses, brushes, and mirrors.

I wish you could see my favorite of all of the treasures—the one item I could hardly wait to lift out of the tissue paper from deep within the bottom compartment of the trunk. It is my great-grandmother's cream-colored, raw silk wedding dress. Included in that part of the chest are the lace-trimmed bloomers and petticoats that she wore under her skirt. We loved to try on the pair of cream high-heeled shoes, each with a satin bow over the toe. There is even a beautiful shawl made out of cream-colored silk to match her dress, with fancy gold plush velvet around the collar. A little note explains that my great-grandmother wore the shawl to ride in the horse-drawn carriage when the wedding was over.

After my grandmother finished telling us the stories, we would carefully pack up the trunk to be stored for another day. That was the mark of a good keeper. First, accepting the responsibility to care for something precious, and, second, knowing that there are certain actions you have to perform to keep those precious things safe. My grandma was a keeper of the stories and memories in that trunk. She was a protector, a guard, and a steward.

Now the trunk is in my family room, and I have become the keeper for a time. I learned what it meant to be a keeper from my grandmother's example. After she died, I accepted the responsibility, and I act according to the lessons that she taught me. I am careful with all of the memories; they are precious to me, because they were precious to her. Sometimes, on different afternoons, I will go through the trunk with my sisters, cousins, and daughters. We remember the stories together, and in doing so, we remember our Grandma Belle.

You may not have realized it yet, but you are a keeper of something very valuable too. Each week you are reminded of this amazing responsibility. See if these words sound familiar to you . . .

" . . . as we come to accept and act upon these values . . ."

Remember the definition of a good keeper? First, *accepting* the responsibility to care for something precious, and, second, knowing that there are certain *actions* you have to perform to keep those precious things safe. The Young Women theme reminds us each week that we can choose to *accept* and *act upon* something very precious. In doing so, we become keepers of the Young Women values.

Throughout all the ages of time there have been righteous women who were keepers. We can learn from their stories as we read through the scriptures. They can become a guide for those of us who live today. The stories portray examples of women who knew how to *accept* and *act upon* precious values. In their day, their effort to live these values allowed them to stand as witnesses of Jesus Christ. In our day, their witness remains. These women are "teachers of good things; that they may teach the young women to be . . . keepers" (Titus 2:3–5).

We can learn much from these stewards who have become protectors of these values, caretakers over essential truths, and guards against the evils of our day—women who knew what it meant to be keepers. You will find eight of their stories within the pages of this book. Reading their stories can help us learn how to accept and act upon values that will become precious to us. As we choose to accept and act upon these values we will find ourselves becoming the kind of women they were—keepers of what matters most.

Keep·er [kee–per] Someone who protects, guards, or looks after something that is important, precious, or valuable.

We are daughters of our Heavenly Father,
who loves us, and we love Him.
We will "stand as witnesses of God at all times
and in all things, and in all places" (Mosiah 18:9) as we strive to live
the Young Women values, which are:

Faith

Divine Nature

Individual Worth

Knowledge

Choice and Accountability

Good Works

Integrity

and Virtue

We believe as we come to accept and act upon these values,
we will be prepared to strengthen home and family,
make and keep sacred covenants,
receive the ordinances of the temple,
and enjoy the blessings of exaltation.

Get ready!

You are about to begin an adventure that could change your life. Let's start things off by taking a short quiz that will help you to learn more about the real you—who you are, and, more importantly, who you would like to become. This is a chance for you to look at the Young Women values in a whole new way. It will help you to determine which of these values you relate to the most, and which ones you want to know more about.

In the general Young Women broadcast in April 2009, Elaine Dalton talked about her love of the Young Women values. She said, "When I was a young woman, my Young Women leaders had each of us choose a symbol that would represent the life that we would live and what we would strive to become as daughters of God. We then stitched these symbols onto our bandlos—which were fabric sashes that we wore. These bandlos were our personal banners to the world! I chose the symbol of a white rose because roses become more and more beautiful as they grow and blossom, and I chose the color white for purity." Then Sister Dalton extended an invitation to young women everywhere: "I encourage each of you to ponder what your personal banner would be if you could give one message to the world."

My Message   My Moment

In the days following that address I talked with many of the young women in my ward. I was surprised to find that each of them had been intrigued by Sister Dalton's invitation. They wanted a chance to determine for themselves what their message to the world would be. It is an invitation that causes reflection and requires pondering. I wonder if you might like to take a minute to think about what your message to the world might be?

This is your chance!

As you take this quiz, think about these questions:

❋ What is my message?

❋ When are the moments that I can share my message?

❋ How can I be a witness to the world as I live my message?

❋ How will living that message help me to understand my inner worth?

My Witness   My Worth

Here we go!

This is the first part of the quiz. Circle the list of words that describes you best. If there are two lists that sound like you, go ahead and circle both of them.

One

Distinct
Personal
Special
Original
Unique
Valuable
Significant

Two

Wise
Observant
Sensitive
Searching
Interested
Perceptive
Questioning

Three

Trustworthy
Believing
Confident
Hopeful
Optimistic
Assured
Loyal

Four

Holy
Sacred
Blessed
Spiritual
Gifted
Creative
Talented

Five

Decisive
Responsible
Dependable
Obedient
Attentive
Observant
Willing

Seven

Kind
Thoughtful
Considerate
Generous
Helpful
Soft-hearted
Tender

Six

Noble
Pure
Strong
Courageous
Devoted
Innocent
Spotless

Eight

Full of Honor
Sincere
Trustworthy
Consistent
Constant
Devoted
Determined

Are you ready for the next step?

Circle the statement that is most like you, or circle the statement that is most like who you want to become. If you like, you can circle two.

1. You are not afraid to act as an instrument in the Lord's hands because you know that He will use you for good. You have learned to pray that the Lord will trust you with specific responsibilities and that you will be able to achieve sucess in carrying out these responsibilities.

2. When you have an opportunity to share what you know, you do it. Sometimes you share your favorite scripture. You like to have conversations about what you learned at church or in seminary.

3. You believe that you are a daughter of a Heavenly Father who loves you. You know that He has a plan for you and that He will help you accomplish what you were sent here to do. You have learned to recognize His hand in your life. You remember to watch for His tender mercies every day.

4   You spend time trying to discover the gifts that Heavenly Father has blessed you with by reading the scriptures, praying, and preparing for a patriarchal blessing. You use the gifts that Heavenly Father has given you to bless the lives of others.

5   You dare to set high standards and choose to defend them. You know how to make good decisions. You are dependable.

6   You seek after things that are virtuous, praiseworthy, and of good report. If it won't strengthen your testimony of Christ, you walk away from it.

7   You love to be on the Lord's errand—you serve just as He would if He were here.

8   You are true in every situation—even when no one is watching. You know what is right and you do it. You are consistent.

Let's keep going.

These instructions are similar to the ones you just finished, but read carefully—the statements are all different. Circle the statement that is most like you, or circle the statement that is most like who you want to become. If you like, you can circle two.

1   You realize that you have been sent to Earth with a divine mission that is yours to achieve. You believe that Heavenly Father will allow you daily experiences that will help you to fulfill that mission. You know what it means to make every moment count.

2   You enjoy obtaining knowledge by study and by faith. You find joy in learning new things in every area of your life. You try to make sure that everything that goes into your mind is good and that it makes you feel good inside.

3   Your life is focused on your belief in Jesus Christ. You have learned to recognize His voice as you read the scriptures, live worthy to hear promptings from the Spirit, and study the words of His servants.

4   You believe that Heavenly Father has given each of us special gifts. You have learned to celebrate and appreciate the gifts from Heavenly Father that make you special. You enjoy being unique.

5   You believe that agency, or the power to make our own choices, is a gift and you cherish it. You know that it is your choice to be known as someone who obeys the Lord. You believe that every action has a consequence, whether for good or for bad. You are good at thinking through the consequences before you make a choice.

6   You have learned to let your thoughts and actions be determined by the strength of your high moral standards. You know that strength comes from purity. You believe that if you are worthy you will be strong.

7   You believe that serving others is important. You enjoy serving everyone around you. You are good at recognizing someone in need, and you always know how to help. You have learned that simple acts of service can help to lead others to Christ.

8   You understand that it is important to be true at all times in whatsoever thing you are entrusted (see Alma 53:20). Your actions are determined by what you know is right and because of this, people have learned to trust you.

Now, take a minute to look at your answers.

Each number will match up to a corresponding value. For example, the statements that are labeled with a number 1 go with individual worth, and the statements next to a number 2 go with knowledge. Take a minute to write the value next to each of the statements you circled. Use the following list to help you keep things straight.

1 = individual worth

2 = knowledge

3 = faith

4 = divine nature

5 = choice and accountability

6 = virtue

7 = good works

8 = integrity

Results

※ Maybe you circled the same number on every single page—if so, you must be really interested in that value. As you read through the rest of the book, pay special attention to the chapter that focuses on that value. Think about why that value is so important to you and how you can incorporate the qualities of that value into every part of your life.

※ Perhaps you circled a different number on every page. That is exciting! Try to

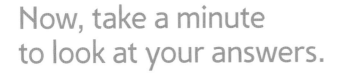

So many different values . . . so mar

discover something new about each of those values as you read through the chapters of this book. Find ways to make those qualities a part of who you are and who you want to become.

❋ There may be some numbers that you didn't mark at all. As you read through those chapters, try to learn something new about that value that you didn't know before. How would living that value make you a better person?

Those who are willing to reflect these colors in a world filled with darkness create a remarkable beauty that arches across the stormy skies of a wicked world—a rainbow whose colors illuminate a path full of promise that stretches throughout eternity.

Which colors stand out to you?
Which do you want to know more about?

As you read through the values in this book, take some time to ponder your message to the world. On the last page of every chapter you will be able to write about your message, your moment, your witness, and your worth. This will allow you to think about each value and its personal meaning to you. Let the colors of these values fill your life, creating a rainbow within, a reminder of your covenant to stand as His witness by becoming a keeper of what matters most.

nique colors . . . so many things to discover . . .

"... women have their roots in the ground, and often those roots are starved and ravaged, yet there is not a human alive who cannot reach and touch, with ... her fingers, the very top of God's rainbow."

—OG MANDINO

I am a daughter of Heavenly Father, who loves me.

I have faith in His eternal plan, which centers on

Jesus Christ, my Savior.

Keeper of

Trustworthy   Believing   Confident

Faith

Full of Conviction   Hopeful   Optimistic

Abish—Keeper of Faith

One of my favorite Book of Mormon heroes is a Lamanite girl named Abish. I don't know how old she was, but I like to imagine she was just your age. Abish had been converted unto the Lord for many years. She learned to believe in the Lord after hearing the testimony of her father. But she never told anyone about her testimony.

Abish was a servant who worked in the home of King Lamoni. Ammon, a Nephite missionary, had been teaching King Lamoni about the gospel. One day, as the king was listening to Ammon speak, he became so overwhelmed with what he had learned that he fell to the earth as if he were dead. For three days he lay there without moving, and finally King Lamoni's wife called for Ammon to tell her what she should do. There were many people who thought the king had died, but the king's wife did not believe that he had. Ammon reassured her that the king was not dead. The next day the king arose and testified of the Lord. Then Ammon, the king, his wife, and his servants all cried unto the Lord, and this time they were all so overwhelmed by the Spirit, they all fell to the earth.

Everyone except for Abish.

After watching all of this happen, Abish wondered if this might be an opportunity to do some missionary work—maybe if other people saw what had happened it would help them to believe in God. The scriptures tell us, "Therefore she ran forth from house to house, making it known unto the people" (Alma 19:17). I love that in her great excitement, she ran.

And so the Lamanite people gathered together in the home of the king. They didn't know what to think. It looked as though everyone were dead. The people thought Ammon had murdered everyone, and they began to murmur amongst themselves. They were angry. One man drew his sword; others called Ammon a monster. There was a lot of contention. After all of Abish's excitement, things were not going well. I wonder if Abish regretted her decision to gather all of the people and share what she believed. The scriptures tell us that when Abish saw the contention, "she was exceedingly sorrowful, even unto tears" (Alma 19:28).

I wonder if she was afraid.

It was a moment of decision for Abish. The easy choice would have been to join with the others and completely ignore what she knew to be true. The hard choice was to be true to what she knew in her heart and to stand up for what she believed. I am sure it was a difficult choice, but Abish had faith. She walked over to the queen and took her by the hand, and as soon as Abish touched her hand, the queen arose. The queen then took King Lamoni by the hand, and King Lamoni testified of what had happened. And everyone who heard his words believed and received a testimony. All of their hearts were changed, and part of that miraculous conversion was due to the fact that Abish remained true to what she believed and wasn't afraid to show it.

"*Faith is not to have a perfect knowledge of things; therefore if ye have faith ye hope for things which are not seen, which are true*" (Alma 32:21).

What do you believe?

Faith is powerful. It is the essence of all of our beliefs.

Have you ever noticed that there are some things we believe in that are so commonplace we sometimes forget about them? Things like believing the sun will rise every morning, that tulips will poke their heads through the soft, warm dirt as the snow begins to disappear, or that school will start again in the fall.

Another way we can understand faith is by looking at relationships. Do you know someone who will never let you down, no matter what? Maybe your mom or dad, your grandma, or your best friend? Someone who is on your side, who cares about you, someone who has got your back? Having faith in someone is believing that they will always be there for you.

Sometimes we have faith in something that we can't see or touch. We have faith in a Heavenly Father who loves us, in our Savior, Jesus Christ, and in many other sacred things.

Faith can be a feeling, whispering something you know to be true.

Faith is real, and the more you believe in something, the more real your faith will become.

What it isn't . . .

Constantly **doubting.**

Living in **fear.**

Not **trusting.**

Acting **disloyal** or **untrue.**

Disbelieving.

What it is . . .

Having complete **trust**
or **confidence** in someone
or something.

Daring to
believe.

Knowing that
something is **real.**

Recently 14,000 youth gathered to celebrate the building of two new temples in Utah. The gathering was held at the Conference Center in downtown Salt Lake City.

What faith looks like today

With great anticipation, the youth filled the Conference Center and waited for the celebration to begin. A few minutes before the event was to start the entire congregation stood to welcome President Thomas S. Monson as he entered the room. In the reverent silence, from the middle section of the farthest balcony a small group of young women begin to quietly sing,

We thank thee, O God, for a prophet
To guide us in these latter days.
We thank thee for sending the gospel
To lighten our minds with its rays.
We thank thee for every blessing
Bestowed by thy bounteous hand.
We feel it a pleasure to serve thee,
And love to obey thy command.

Others surrounding them joined in the song, until, like a wave coursing through the Conference Center, each of the youth there joined the singing, expressing their testimony, sharing their faith through song.

All it took was a small handful of girls to unite a group of youth, 14,000 strong, into sharing what they believed.

What do you have the power to do?

Dare to share your faith and find out.

"I may be **one**,
but **one** becomes **two**,
when **you** stand with **me**,
and **I** stand with **you** . . ."

—HILARY WEEKS ("I WILL" LYRICS)

Accept Faith

Heavenly Father loves you.

He has miracles in store for you.

He knows you by name.

He sent His Son to help you make it back home.

You can learn to recognize His voice as you read the scriptures, live worthy to hear promptings from the Spirit, and study the words of His servants.

Believe it.

Act Upon Faith

Obtain your own testimony that you are a daughter of Heavenly Father who loves you, knows you, and has a plan for you.

Keep a journal of the times when you hear His voice.

Trust in Him.

Let yourself believe.

Set a goal to study the scriptures and pray every day.

Write down the moments when you see His hand in your life.

Find opportunities to testify to your family and your friends.

"When you come to the end of all the light you know, and it's time to step into the darkness of the unknown, faith is knowing that one of two things shall happen: Either you will be given something solid to stand on or you will be taught to fly." —EDWARD TELLER

faith

What is my message of faith?

~~~~~~

~~~~~~

When are the moments that I can
share my message?

~~~~~~

~~~~~~

My Message   My Moment

How can I be a witness to the world
as I live my message?

~~~~~~

~~~~~~

How will living that message help me
to understand my inner worth?

~~~~~~

~~~~~~

My Witness   My Worth

I have inherited divine qualities,
which I will strive to develop.

Keeper of

Blessed   Spiritual   Becoming Holy

Divine Nature

Creative   Gifted   Talented

Lois and Eunice—
Keepers of Divine Nature

Somewhere deep inside you, hidden within your soul and nestled inside your heart, are gifts that come from your Heavenly Father. As you learn to discover these gifts, you will be led to understand your divine nature.

In the book of Timothy, one of the chapters records a conversation between Paul and young Timothy. Paul tells Timothy, "Let no man despise thy youth; but be thou an example of the believers, in word, in conversation, in charity, in spirit, in faith, in purity" (1 Timothy 4:12). Then Paul gives Timothy another important piece of advice: "Neglect not the gift that is in thee" (1 Timothy 4:14).

Have you ever wondered what the gift was that Timothy had been given? We find out in 2 Timothy 1:5–6 when Paul tells Timothy that he is filled with joy every time he calls to remembrance "the *unfeigned faith* that is in thee, which dwelt first in thy grandmother Lois, and thy mother Eunice; and I am persuaded that in thee also. Wherefore I put thee in remembrance that thou *stir up the gift of God,* which is in thee" (emphasis added). Timothy's gift was faith. I love that Timothy's gift of faith was also a gift that could be seen in his grandmother, Lois, and in his mother, Eunice.

In 2 Timothy 3:15 Paul tells us that "from a child [Timothy had] known the holy scriptures." I feel certain that his grandmother and mother probably taught him. In doing so, they helped him to discover the divine gifts he had been blessed with, both through their own example and through the words of the scriptures.

Just like Timothy, Heavenly Father will surround us with women who will help us discover our own divine gifts. You might think of your grandmothers, or your mother, but He also calls inspired Young Women leaders who can help you understand the gifts that you have been given.

It is important that we, just like Timothy, stir up the gift that is in us. The Young Women Personal Progress book tells us that we can develop our gifts by being obedient to the commandments and by having personal prayer and daily scripture study.

Take a moment to think about your own mother and grandmother.

What do you love about them?

What are some of the qualities you could learn from them?

Maybe they could teach you dedication, loyalty, or perseverance. Perhaps you, like Timothy, could learn to be faithful. Some women are especially good at listening to the whisperings of the Spirit. You could be someone like that. I know that one of the most precious gifts I have been given is something that I learned from my mother and my grandmothers. It is the gift of compassion, of serving, of learning what it means to give all. When I use that gift, I think of their example.

I want to be like them.

"*Be partakers of the divine nature . . . Giving all diligence, add to your faith virtue; and to virtue knowledge; and to knowledge temperance; and to temperance patience; and to patience godliness; and to godliness brotherly kindness; and to brotherly kindness charity*" (2 PETER 1:4–7).

It's what's inside that really counts.

Think for a minute about diligence, faith, virtue, knowledge, temperance, patience, godliness, kindness, and charity. Did you know that those qualities are considered gifts?

You might be thinking to yourself, Those aren't gifts. That's because we tend to think of a gift as something like a bike, an iPod, or maybe a new pair of jeans. What we think of as a good gift is usually something that you can either touch with your hand or something that has some kind of monetary value, right?

Can a gift be precious if it doesn't have a price tag on it?

This year I had an odd birthday. My husband got called out of town, unexpectedly, to China. He would miss my birthday while he was gone, so we decided to celebrate as a family when he returned home. I went to stay at a cabin in Heber with my mom and dad and the rest of my family for the week. As luck would have it, my mom forgot to bring my birthday gift up to the cabin, and so the day of my birthday came and went, and I almost didn't receive any gifts. Did you notice the word *almost*?

Unexpectedly, late in the evening, three of my nieces, Brooklin, Ella, and Kemry, came with a large pile of papers over to where I was sitting. They had colored page after page with brightly colored crayons. I happened to be featured on every page. There was one with me holding flowers, one with me wearing a crown, one with me with several birds flying around my head (probably pets, I would assume), and finally, on the last page, a huge heart with a simple, handwritten note:

"We jes wanted this too be spishul."

It was the only gift I opened on my birthday this year. It is one of the best gifts I've ever received.

Some of the most precious gifts that have been given to us come from our Father in Heaven. It's what makes us "spishul." They are gifts that are inside of us; they make up who we are; they are divine qualities given to each of us specifically.

Elder Joseph B. Wirthlin spoke of these divine gifts. He counseled, "There is a spark of greatness within every one of us—a gift from our loving and eternal Heavenly Father. What we do with that gift is up to us."

What is your spark of greatness?

What are your gifts?

What will you do with them?

"Your loving Heavenly Father has blessed you with talents and abilities that will help you fulfill your divine mission" (Young Women Personal Progress book).

Choose to be a young woman who is intent on discovering your divine nature by learning to celebrate your God-given gifts. Stir up the gift that is within you. Discover your spark of greatness. You are capable of doing great things with the gift you have been given.

Be willing to try.

What it isn't ...

Feeling like a **nobody.**

Assuming you
are **unimportant.**

Doubting yourself.

Wishing you could be
just like **somebody else.**

What it is . . .

Discovering the gifts that are **unique** to you.

Reaching your **potential.**

Becoming the person Heavenly Father knows you can be.

Knowing that you are special, out of the ordinary, one of a kind.

Adam was different from the other seventh graders, different enough that he didn't have very many friends. He spent most of the time in his special ed class at the school because it was a place that was familiar to him, and the people there were always nice.

What divine nature looks like today

One day Adam and his teacher started talking about the upcoming student council election. Adam told the teacher he had voted for a girl named Sara. The teacher knew who Sara was because Adam talked about her so often.

Sara was an outgoing, happy girl who was always surrounded by people. She was friends with everyone. It didn't matter which group you were in, if you had a class with Sara, you were her friend. And somewhere in her circle she had found room to include Adam. She didn't worry about the ways he was different—she recognized the good in him, and she made him feel important. This was Sara's gift; she always saw the good in people, and she included everyone.

As their conversation ended the teacher asked Adam, "Who do you think will win?"

"Sara," he replied simply, "because she likes everyone.

Even people like me."

"There is **within** each of us a **divine spark** of **greatness**. Who knows of what we are **capable** if we only **try**?"

—JOSEPH B. WIRTHLIN
("THE ABUNDANT LIFE,"
ENSIGN, MAY 2006, 99–102)

Accept Divine Nature

Believe that you are someone important.

Know that you have inherited divine qualities.

Celebrate the gifts from Heavenly Father that are unique to you.

You don't have to be just like somebody else . . .

Be You!

Act Upon
Divine Nature

Use your gifts to bless the lives of others.

Stir up the gift that is in you.

Remember, you are a daughter of God.

Make a list of your gifts to keep as a reminder.

You are capable of doing great things.

Discover your spark of greatness.

Neglect not YOUR gift.

"You are what you always imagined you could be . . .

. . . See it."

—STEPHANIE SMITH MABEY
("YOUR LIGHT" LYRICS)

divine nature

What is my message of divine nature?

. . . .

. . . .

When are the moments that I can
share my message?

. . . .

. . . .

My Message   My Moment

How can I be a witness to the world
as I live my message?

. . . .

. . . .

How will living that message help me
to understand my inner worth?

. . . .

. . . .

My Witness   My Worth

I am of infinite worth with my own
divine mission, which I will strive to fulfill.

Keeper of

Unique   Valuable   Distinct

Individual Worth

Special   Significant   Important

Esther—Keeper of Individual Worth

I love the story of Esther because it reminds me of a fairy tale. Go find a comfy spot to sit in, and I will tell it to you.

Once there was a Jewish orphan named Esther. She was raised by her uncle, Mordecai, and he loved her very much. One day the fair young maidens in all the provinces of the kingdom were gathered to a palace where they would prepare to meet the king and be considered to become the queen.

After months of preparation, every maiden came unto the king. In the kingdom there were many rules, and one of the rules was that no one could talk to the king unless he called for her by name. The penalty for breaking this rule was death, so each of the maidens waited in the palace until her name was called. When it was Esther's turn she went up unto the king. He loved Esther above all women, and so he made her the queen.

One day a terrible thing happened. The king's advisor, Haman, who was a bad man, told all of the people they had to bow before him. Mordecai, Esther's uncle, refused to bow before this evil man. This made Haman furious. Haman talked the king into sending out a decree that all of the Jews in the land should be killed.

Queen Esther was afraid for Mordecai and for all of her people. She didn't know what to do, so she sent one of her servants to ask Mordecai's advice. Mordecai told Queen Esther to tell the king that she was a Jew and ask him to save her people.

But Esther was scared. Remember the rule of the kingdom? Esther had not been called in to see the king. Mordecai knew how dangerous this would be. He had raised

Esther as his daughter, and he loved her. But still, he gave Esther great counsel: "Who knoweth whether thou art come to the kingdom for *such* a time as this?" (Esther 4:14).

Now, that may have been true, but it didn't make it less scary. After much thought, Esther sent her servant back to Mordecai with her answer: "Go, gather together all the Jews . . . and fast ye for me, and neither eat nor drink three days, night or day: I also and my maidens will fast likewise; and so will I go in unto the king, which is not according to the law: and if I perish, I perish" (Esther 4:16).

Queen Esther decided to be brave and fulfill her divine mission, knowing that it might mean she would die. But Esther did not go into the king alone. Mordecai and all of the Jews were fasting for her. And she and all of her best friends were fasting. Queen Esther approached the king knowing that the strength of her people, her friends, and, most importantly, the Lord was with her.

On the third day, Esther put on her fancy, royal clothing and stood in the inner court of the king's house while the king sat upon his royal throne. When the king saw Esther, standing all dressed up in the middle of the court, he remembered how much he loved her, and he raised his golden scepter. Esther came to him and touched the top of the scepter, and she was allowed to speak without being put to death.

The king asked, "What wilt thou, queen Esther? and what is thy request?" (Esther 5:3). Queen Esther told the King she was a Jew, and begged him to save her life and the life of her people. Then Esther told the king that his servant was a wicked man. So Haman, the evil man, was put to death, and Esther and her people were saved.

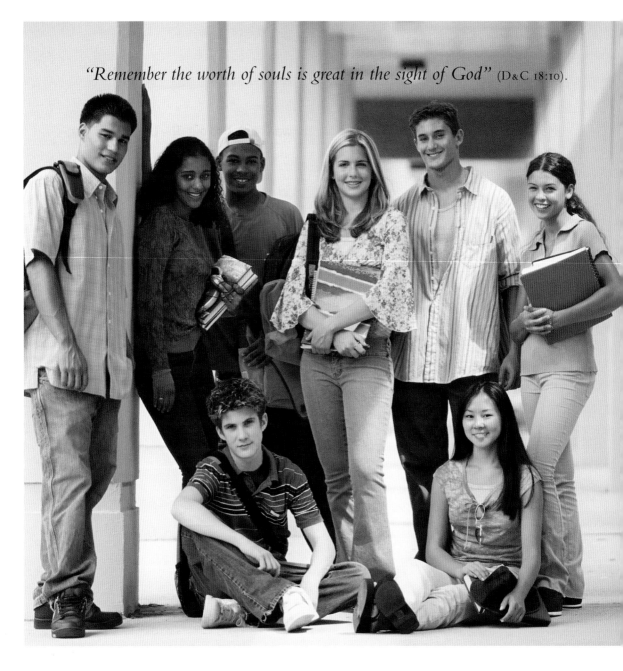

"Remember the worth of souls is great in the sight of God" (D&C 18:10).

What is your mission?

Maybe you already know; perhaps you are still waiting to find out. The Lord knows just how He wants to use each of us, and if we listen to the promptings of the Spirit we will be guided in the direction we need to go. Part of our mission might include life-changing events just like Queen Esther had. But most often we will fulfill our mission in the actions we perform every day. I have learned that if I pray every morning, expressing my willingness to be on the Lord's errand, He will give me a mission to perform that day.

Sometimes the mission might be as simple as visiting a friend or sitting by someone we don't know. Other times we might be prompted to help someone in need. More often than not, the action we are called upon to perform will require us to make a decision—we have to decide whether or not we will do it. Sometimes we might be scared to talk to someone new. Or maybe we feel like we don't have time in our schedule for what the Lord is asking. It can be hard to decide if we are willing to fulfill the Lord's mission for us that day. But I have learned that when I do what the Lord asks me to do, He gives me the opportunity to be a part of small miracles in the ordinary moments of my life.

What it isn't . . .

Walking away from things
that are **hard.**

Turning away from
life-changing opportunities because
of **fear.**

Expecting that if you won't do it,
somebody else will.

What it is . . .

Believing that your actions
are **significant.**

Understanding that what you have to
offer is **valuable.**

Realizing that you were **prepared**
for this **moment** in time.

On the first day of seminary during my junior year of high school, our teacher, Brother Howell, gave each of us a mission to accomplish. He wanted us to make a new friend. We could choose anyone in our class—it just had to be someone we didn't already know. I chose Kevin.

What individual worth looks like today

Kevin was different from the other kids in our class. He wore the same clothes every day—a white oxford shirt, a pair of levis, and black slip-on shoes. He had a beautiful voice—it was really deep—and he sang every song . . . loud.

The first month I waited for him outside the door of the school and walked with him across the parking lot and into the seminary building. Sometimes I would sit by him in seminary. This plan allowed me to accomplish the mission Brother Howell had given me but not be seen with Kevin outside of seminary.

Then Kevin started looking for me in the halls and at lunch. He would yell my name as loud as he could—just like he sang the hymns. My friends were embarrassed. They didn't want to walk down the hall with me for fear of seeing Kevin. I found myself having to make a really hard choice: Was I really Kevin's friend or not?

It was a difficult decision. I didn't want to create any hard feelings with my friends, but the commitment I had made to Brother Howell nagged at the back of my mind.

After thinking it through, I realized that it wasn't just a mission to fulfill anymore. I liked Kevin. He was my friend.

One day toward the end of school, I was standing at my locker grabbing my books for second period, and I was running late. Just as I was shutting my locker, Kevin and his two friends came around the corner. He said, "Hey! I'm on a scavenger hunt and I need to borrow one of your shoes."

I looked down at my feet. I was wearing sandals, so if I let Kevin borrow one of my shoes my foot would be completely bare. The bell was about to ring, so I had to make a quick decision. Finally I replied, "OK, you can take my shoe. But you HAVE to bring it back before second period ends. I am not going to walk around with one bare foot all day."

I will never forget what happened next. Just as I reached down to take the sandal off, Kevin stopped me and said, "It's all right, I don't really need your shoe." Then he turned to his two friends and said, "See, I told you there was one person in this school who believed in me."

Immediately the thought came into my mind: "What if I had said no?"

I am so glad I didn't. On that day my mission was just to believe in my new friend. To trust him. It was so simple. In that small moment I began to understand how it felt to be on the Lord's errand, to believe in someone just as He would have if He had been there.

"God does notice us, and he **watches over us**. But it is usually through **another person** that he meets our **needs**."

—SPENCER W. KIMBALL
("SMALL ACTS OF SERVICE,"
ENSIGN, DECEMBER 1974, 5).

Accept Individual Worth

Realize that you have been sent to earth with a divine mission that is yours to achieve.

Believe that Heavenly Father will allow you daily experiences that will help you to fulfill that mission.

If you want to discover the mission the Lord needs you to fulfill today, just ask.

Learn to listen to the whisperings of the Spirit.

Be on His errand.

Act Upon
Individual Worth

Be on the Lord's errand. He will use you for good.

This is your moment.

Come take your place.

Be who the Lord needs you to be.

Make every moment count.

You can do hard things.

Believe in yourself!

. . . .

"I will prepare and someday my chance will come."

—ABRAHAM LINCOLN

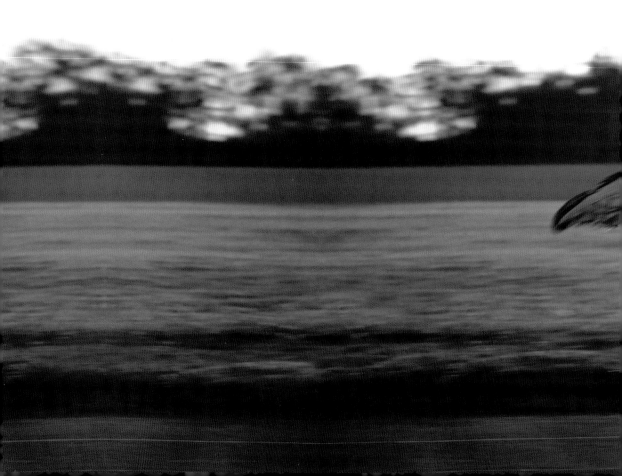

individual worth

What is my message of individual worth?

When are the moments that I can share my message?

My Message   My Moment

How can I be a witness to the world
as I live my message?

How will living that message help me
to understand my inner worth?

My Witness   My Worth

I will continually seek opportunities

for learning and growth.

Keeper of

Observant   Searching   Interested

Knowledge

Perceptive   Questioning   Wise

Mary—Keeper of Knowledge

Sometimes when I read the scriptures I like to ask myself a question: *Could this be my story?* Then I try to imagine myself in that situation, as if I were there. What would I have felt, or thought, or decided to do if it had been my experience? It makes my scripture reading much more exciting.

We can try it with the story of Mary and her sister, Martha. Here's how the story goes. One day as Christ was traveling, He went to a certain village to the home of a certain woman. *Certain* is a particularly important word in this story, and it tells us that the Savior knew exactly where He was going and exactly who He wanted to see—a certain woman, in a certain village. That woman happened to be Martha, and she had a sister whose name was Mary.

On this particular day Martha was distracted. The scriptures tell us she was busy serving. I imagine she was probably throwing together a quick dinner for her unexpected guest. As she worked, her younger sister sat at the feet of the Lord, forgetting everything else but Him.

And so Martha served, and Mary sat at the Lord's feet and listened to Him teach. After a while Martha asked the Savior if Mary should come and help her. The Savior's reply is very important. He doesn't tell Martha to stop serving, and He doesn't tell Mary to stop listening. He simply let Martha know that what Mary was doing was fine. He replied, "Mary hath chosen that good part, which shall not be taken away from her" (Luke 10:42).

Now, if we were to ask ourselves, "Could this be my story?" what would we discover?

Let's pretend we are Mary. The first thing we know is that her house was a place the Savior felt comfortable visiting. Now I want you to think about where you live, particularly your bedroom. Think of the music you listen to, the stuff that hangs on your walls, the conversations you have there. Is it a place where the Savior would feel comfortable visiting?

We also know from this story that Mary set aside everything she was doing to sit at the feet of the Lord and listen to Him. Do you ever do that? Setting aside time for scripture study, making seminary a priority, attending all three meetings at church, and saying morning and evening prayers all count as moments at the feet of the Lord.

Last, we are taught that when Mary chose to learn from the Lord, she chose that good part. How can we do that? Think about how you learn. Anytime you put something into your mind, you are learning. Obviously when you go to school you learn. But have you ever considered that when you listen to music, watch a movie, or read a book you are also taking information into your mind? That means you are learning. Do you do what Mary did? Do you choose the good part?

"Seek learning, even by study and also by faith" (D&C 88:118).

Surround yourself with knowledge.

When I was a senior in high school, our family moved to another state. Moving is hard. I will be honest, there were some days that I was discouraged. Sometimes I cried. To help me rise above the sad times my mom let me do something that most moms would never agree to. I started taping quotes on my bedroom walls. At first it was the handouts I got from Young Women. But then I bought special paper so I could write down any uplifting message I found and hang it up on the walls. Some of the pages contained scriptures. Some had thoughts or quotes. Others had snippets from movies or lyrics from popular songs. I had only one requirement—the words had to be positive, uplifting, and motivational. I wrote them down and hung them where I could see them every day, in hopes that I would remember them.

By the time I graduated, the quotes filled all four walls of my bedroom, floor to ceiling. There were so many pieces of paper you could no longer see the color of the paint on my bedroom walls. And an interesting thing happened: I noticed that people loved to come sit in my room. When they were sad or lonely, they would come. When they were searching for a much-needed quote or were writing a talk or a paper, they would visit. Sometimes they came for advice—not from me, from my walls. Even when I wasn't there, people would come and sit in my room. I think they were drawn to the "good parts," and they felt uplifted when they read them—just like I did.

When we surround ourselves with good things that are positive and uplifting, we are obtaining the right kind of knowledge. Just like Mary, we are choosing the good part.

What it isn't . . .

Believing that learning is defined by a 4.0 or a letter grade.

Lacking **understanding.**

Being **unaware** or foolish.

Disbelieving.

Displaying your
ignorance.

What it is . . .

Sharing **talents, accomplishments,** or **skills** gained by experience.

Receiving **insight** into something you are studying.

Practicing **abilities** that are new.

Learning. Understanding. Knowing.

A young woman living in Lima, Peru, heard the counsel that she ought to be having family home evening, but she was the only member in her family, and she was just seventeen years old.

What knowledge looks like today

One Sunday somebody bore a particularly strong testimony about family home evening and she decided she would begin holding family home evening on her own. She went home that very day and sat in her living room. She sang a song, had a prayer, and began to have a lesson. Her family made fun of her, particularly her two older brothers. They laughed at her, jeered, and asked her what she was doing as a Mormon. In tears she fled to her bedroom, where she finished the lesson that night.

The following Monday, in spite of the resistance she had encountered from her family the previous week, she went ahead and had family home evening by herself again. The next Monday she did the same thing. On the third Monday something remarkable happened. As she began singing the opening song, there was a knock on her door. Her older brother said, "Mary, may I come in? I really would like to know what you are doing." She said, "Well, yes, if you're not going to make fun of me." They sang, prayed, and learned together. The following week the second brother joined them.

Some time later she bore her testimony in stake conference. She said, "And here," pointing to one of the front rows, "are my parents and both of those brothers. They are all members of the Church now."

What a tremendous blessing! By singing, praying, and *learning,* this seventeen-year-old girl, through obedience to the commandments, was the instrument by which her whole family was converted. The Lord can work miracles through men, women, children, and, yes, even through teenagers. (As told by Elder Gene R. Cook in *Raising Up a Family to the Lord*, [Salt Lake City: Deseret Book, 1993], 263–64.)

". . . the **beautiful** thing—perhaps the thing
I **love** most about the gospel—is that everything we
learn we can use and take with us and use it again.
No bit of **knowledge** goes wasted.
Everything you are **learning** now is
preparing you for something else.
Did you know that?
What a concept!"

—MARJORIE PAY HINCKLEY
(*SMALL AND SIMPLE THINGS*,
[SALT LAKE CITY: DESERET BOOK,
2003], 138)

Accept Knowledge

Knowledge can be gathered from every situation you are in.

You can acquire knowledge by study *and* by faith.

Everything that enters your mind is knowledge—that includes the things you read, the movies you watch, the music you listen to, and the conversations you are a part of.

Don't allow anything into your mind that shouldn't be there.

Choose the good part.

Act Upon Knowledge

Find joy from learning new things all through your life.

Don't be afraid to share what you know.

Next time you and your friends are trying to think of something to talk about, share your favorite scripture, and ask them theirs.

Ask someone's opinion about a gospel subject you have been wondering about.

Try having a conversation with someone about something you learned at church or in seminary.

Find the good.

"*Knock* . . . and ask your heart
what it doth *know.*"

—WILLIAM SHAKESPEARE

knowledge

What is my message of knowledge?

~~~~~~

~~~~~~

When are the moments that I can share my message?

~~~~~~

~~~~~~

My Message   My Moment

How can I be a witness to the world
as I live my message?

~~~~~~

~~~~~~

How will living that message help me
to understand my inner worth?

~~~~~~

~~~~~~

My Witness   My Worth

I will choose good over evil and
will accept responsibility for my decisions.

Keeper of

Responsible   Dependable   Obedient

Choice and Accountability

Attentive   Willing   Observant

The daughters of Shallum—
Keepers of Choice and Accountability

I want to tell you two stories about making choices. Lehonti, king of the Lamanites, was on top of a high mountain. Amalickiah wanted to trick the king, kill him, and become the new king. He tried to convince Lehonti to come down from the mountain where he was safe. But Lehonti said no. Three times Amalickiah asked Lehonti to come down and talk to him, and three times Lehonti said no. The fourth time Amalickiah came part of the way up the mountain and asked Lehonti to come only that far. So Lehonti came down the mountain. He didn't lower his standards all the way—just a little bit. It was a bad choice. But Lehonti didn't know it was a bad choice because Amalickiah pretended to be his friend. And slowly, after many days, Amalickiah poisoned Lehonti by degrees, and Lehonti died. It is a terrible ending. Here is the second story, I think you will like it better.

Jerusalem was in bad shape. The walls had been broken down. It was not a safe place. Nehemiah was worried and he prayed for direction. The Lord told him to re-build the wall, so he gathered the people together and began to work. Meanwhile, the enemies of Jerusalem laughed and said, "What is this thing that ye do?" And Nehemiah answered, "God . . . will prosper us; therefore we his servants will arise and build" (Nehemiah 2:19-20).

Many people decided to help Nehemiah build the wall, including the men of Jericho, the goldsmiths, and the merchants. The scriptures list more than forty-five other men who wanted to help build. And then, in Nehemiah 3:12, we read about

Shallum, son of Halohesh, the ruler of the half part of Jerusalem, *and his daughters.* I love to think about Shallum's daughters. Their father must have been a very important man. I wonder if these girls were used to being waited upon, if perhaps they had servants who attended to their every need. But that didn't stop them. They worked shoulder to shoulder with all of those men and built the wall to protect what was most important to them.

The wicked men continued to conspire against the people who were building the wall. So Nehemiah gathered the people together. He armed them with weapons and told them, "Be not ye afraid of them: remember the Lord" (Nehemiah 4:14). And so they built the wall with one hand and carried a weapon with them in the other. That must have been hard. When the enemy found out that the people continued to work, they asked Nehemiah to come down from what he was doing and meet with them. Sound familiar? And he replied, "I am doing a great work, so that I cannot come down" (Nehemiah 6:3). Four times the enemy asked Nehemiah to come down, and every time he answered them the same. Finally, the fifth time they sent Nehemiah a letter and tried to make him feel afraid. But he replied, "Should such a man as I flee?" (Nehemiah 6:11).

Nehemiah was different from Lehonti. He knew what his standards were, *and* he was willing to protect them. His reply to the enemy was not just no. Do you remember what he said? "I am doing a great work, so that I cannot come down." Nehemiah and his people, including Shallum's daughters, had made their choice, and they would not come down for anything. In verses 15–16 we read, "So the wall was finished . . . [and] when all our enemies heard thereof . . . they perceived that this work was wrought of our God" (Nehemiah 6:15–16).

"Choose you this day whom ye will serve; . . . but as for me and my house, we will serve the Lord" (JOSHUA 24:15).

Choose to be a builder.

I love to think of Shallum's daughters when I read this story. Working side by side with Nehemiah and hundreds of others to protect what mattered most to them—one hand building, one hand ready to defend, with a determination to stand fast for what they believed. Even when the enemy laughed and mocked them, and threatened to destroy them, they believed that God would strengthen them. They were not afraid; they were doing a great work.

They made their choice and they stuck with it until the end.

The Personal Progress book encourages us to do just what the daughters of Shallum did—to find strength as we work side by side with the young men and our families. It encourages us to review the standards in the *For the Strength of Youth* pamphlet. "Commit to live them. As you do this your example will strengthen your family and the young men and young women with whom you associate" (Young Women Personal Progress, 2).

Working shoulder to shoulder we will strengthen one another, building with one hand and defending with the other. And then when the enemy questions our determination we will reply, "Should such [women] as we are flee?"

Never.

What it isn't . . .

Acting **irresponsibly** or **untrustworthily.**

Faltering, wavering, or being indecisive.

Becoming **wishy-washy.**

Changing constantly.

What it is . . .

Choosing the best course of **action.**

Accepting **responsibility** for **actions** and **decisions.**

Selecting **carefully.**

Deciding between **good** and evil.

In our family when we talk about choices and accountability and having consequences for our actions, we can't help but remember Caleb's hundred-dollar day.

What choice and accountability look like today

One day two of Caleb's friends stole his car key during first period. They took the key home and placed it in boiling hot Jell-O, and then they let it set in the refrigerator. When school was over, they presented Caleb with his key, stuck right in the middle of a big bowl of Jell-O.

Later that afternoon Caleb was telling me all about the experience. Then he said, "Don't worry, Mom, I'm getting them back. I stole Anne Marie's phone and put it in Jell-O."

I just about died! I said, "Caleb, what were you thinking? You can't put a phone in Jell-O."

And he said, "Don't worry, Mom. I put it in a plastic bag first." Somewhat relieved, I asked him if he'd remembered to burp the bag.

Now, if you don't know about burping a Ziploc bag, here is a quick lesson. When you put something with weight into a plastic bag and then into liquid, all of the air must be out of the bag before you close it. Otherwise it will sink to the bottom, and all of the air will try to escape from the bag, and the bag will "burp" itself without you knowing, and fill completely up with whatever liquid is surrounding it. Just ask Caleb.

Caleb didn't know he was supposed to burp the bag. He took the bowl of Jell-O out of the fridge and, sure enough, when we opened up the phone there were

Jell-O bubbles floating across the screen. We took out the battery and placed the entire phone in a bowl of rice (because for some reason that is what you are supposed to do if your phone gets wet)—but it didn't work.

I told Caleb to get a hundred-dollar bill out of the money he had just been paid for work. So, Caleb wrapped up the hundred-dollar bill and refrigerated it in Jell-O instead. Now, don't feel too sorry for Caleb—at least he outdid the pranksters. That night when Anne Marie came to our home, she got *two* bowls—one with a hundred-dollar bill in the middle of Jell-O, and the other with her phone covered in rice.

If you ever find yourself wondering if there are consequences for your actions, just think of Caleb. His hundred-dollar day is a great reminder that even small choices have consequences.

It is important to understand that not all consequences are bad. If you make a bad choice, you will have a bad consequence. But what happens if you make a good choice? Good consequences come from choosing the right.

If you ever wonder if the choice you are about to make is a good one, ask someone. Your mom or dad or one of your leaders will always be happy to help you to know if the choice you are about to make will have a good consequence. Whether it is as simple as a silly prank, or trying to find the courage to stand up for something you believe, your choices are important.

Never **underestimate** the power of **one** good choice.

Accept Choice and Accountability

Agency, or the power to make our own choices, is a gift.

Decide right now that you want to be known as someone who obeys the Lord.

Learn to think about the consequence before you make a choice.

Ask yourself if the decision you are about to make is a good one.

Surround yourself with people who will encourage you to choose the right.

Remember, every action has a consequence, whether for bad or for good.

You choose.

Act Upon
Choice and Accountability

Dare to set your standards and defend them.

Stand fast for what you believe.

Be a builder—fortify yourself, your home, and your family.

Choose the right.

Never flee from doing your duty.

Set your standards high—and don't come down for anything!

"When the time for decision arrives the time for preparation is past."

—THOMAS S. MONSON

choice and accountability

What is my message of choice and accountability?

. . . .

. . . .

When are the moments that I can share my message?

. . . .

. . . .

My Message   My Moment

How can I be a witness to the world
as I live my message?

. . . .

. . . .

How will living that message help me
to understand my inner worth?

. . . .

. . . .

My Witness   My Worth

I will help others and build the kingdom through righteous service.

Keeper of

Kind   Thoughtful   Considerate

Good
Works

Generous   Tender   Soft-hearted

A Great Woman—Keeper of Good Works

One of my favorite stories in the Bible is about a woman whose name we do not know. She is known simply as a great woman.

Here is how the story goes.

Elisha was a prophet of the Lord. Every time he visited the city Shunem, he would pass by the home of a great woman who would offer him bread. One day this great woman said to her husband, "Behold now, I perceive that this is an holy man of God, which passeth by us continually" (2 Kings 4:9).

Right away we learn two things about this woman. First, she knew that Elisha was a holy man, and second, we learn that he came to her house continually. So, if we want to be known as a great woman, what are two things we need to do? Recognize the prophet today as a holy man, and invite him into our house continually. Now, most likely the prophet will not visit your home. But when we listen to general conference or read his words in the *Ensign* or the *New Era,* he is visiting our home, just like Elisha visited the woman in this story.

One day the woman asked her husband if they could make a place for the prophet to stay. Nothing fancy—a little chamber with a bed, a table, a stool, and a candlestick. (It is important to note that what she offered did not require a lot of money, time, or great talent. She simply offered what she had.)

And so the prophet Elisha came and stayed in this chamber she had made and he was grateful. He called for the woman to come to him and he said, "Thou hast been careful for us with all this care; what is to be done for thee?" (2 Kings 4:13). He wondered if he should say good things about her to the king or even to the captain of the host.

But the woman answered, "I dwell among mine own people" (2 Kings 4:13). Or in other words, *I am happy just the way things are and I don't expect anything in return for my service.* In our day, the conversation would have gone something like this. Elisha would have asked, "What can I do to repay you?" And the woman would have replied, "Nothing."

This woman was happy to serve without a reward. I find it fitting that the identity of the woman who performed this quiet act of kindness remains secret today. We know her story, but we are never told her name.

She is known simply as "a great woman."

"*Therefore let your light so shine before this people, that they may see your good works and glorify your Father who is in heaven*" (3 Nephi 12:16).

Give your heart.

Often the greatest acts of service you will perform will go unnoticed by the world at large. Sometimes you may even serve someone in a way that leaves them wondering who you are. In those moments you will be remembered simply as a great woman, and I have learned that this is the best title you could ever hope to receive.

One of the greatest lessons in this scripture story is for us to realize that the woman did the best she could with what she already had. She gave what she could. We can do the same thing. Often the greatest acts of service we can perform will cost us nothing. A great woman is someone who recognizes the need of another—whatever that need may be—and does something about it. Perhaps someone is having a bad day, and all they need is someone who is willing to listen. Saying hi to someone in the hall, or inviting someone to sit with your group at lunch is another way to serve. Sometimes the greatest service comes from someone who is simply willing to be a true friend.

What it isn't . . .

Being **unkind, cruel,** or **mean.**

Acting **harshly** or **selfishly.**

Ignoring a need.

Allowing someone to **hurt** or **suffer.**

What it is . . .

Giving **help.**

Lending a hand.

Being **kindhearted**
and **tender.**

Knowing what it means to **give.**

Showing true **concern**
for another.

It was Christmastime. Torrey, who was serving as the Laurel president in her ward, was listening to the First Presidency Christmas devotional. Her heart was touched as she listened to President Monson describe a class of Laurel girls who had spent an

What good works look like today

evening with a widow in their ward, decorating a tree, baking cookies, and wrapping packages. During his address President Monson encouraged, "There is yet time this year to extend a helping hand, a loving heart, and a willing spirit. In other words, to follow the example set by our Savior and to serve as he would have us serve. . . . Is there someone for whom you should provide service this Christmas? Is there one who awaits your visit?" (Christmas devotional, December 2008).

Immediately after the devotional finished, Torrey called her Young Women president and said, "I felt like the prophet was speaking to me." She took his message to heart and decided to come up with a way that her Laurel class could make a difference in the life of someone that season. Impressed by President Monson's example of caring for the elderly, Torrey contacted a rest home to see if the young women could visit once a week through the month of December. She asked for a list of names of people who would not receive visitors or gifts on Christmas Day. Then the class of fifteen girls went to work. Once a week they visited the rest home, stopping to visit each person. Hoping to earn money to provide gifts for their new friends, Torrey contacted a local business to ask if her Young Women group could clean their facility every week until Christmas. They worked early mornings before the store opened, carefully saving up the money they earned. After the third week, they took their money and went on a shopping spree, purchasing four gifts for each person on their list. On the morning of Christmas Eve, fifteen young women showed up at the rest home, spending the day caroling in each of the rooms, making sure each person was remembered, and giving each resident a donated piece of jewelry or a pair of Christmas socks.

Christmas Day dawned just as it always had, but for Torrey's family, and for several other families in the ward, this Christmas was different. They put their morning celebrations on hold, leaving behind their wrapped presents as they set out first thing for the rest home. That day their celebrations began as they visited the rooms of each person on Torrey's list, dropping off the gifts, and pausing to see the joy on the faces of the recipients as the gift were carefully unwrapped and cherished.

Just as President Monson had promised, it was a memorable season, one they would not forget. Through the counsel of a living prophet they had found an opportunity to bless the lives of others, and within that opportunity they had learned to serve as the Savior would serve.

"There are **hearts to gladden**. . . . **kind words** to say. . . . **gifts** to be given. . . . **deeds to be done.**"

—THOMAS S. MONSON
("THE SEARCH FOR JESUS,"
ENSIGN, DECEMBER 1990, 2)

Accept Good Works

Good works are an important part of leading
others to Christ.

Simple acts of service really can make a difference.
That's why the Savior has asked us to love one another.

Remember the counsel given by President Monson: "Never
postpone a prompting."

Be aware of those around you and try to find a way that you
might be able to serve them.

Give your heart.

Act Upon

Good Works

Comfort another.

Learn to watch for ways that you can serve.

Perform a random act of kindness every day.

Look for someone in need.

Help to bear some-one else's burden.

Never postpone a prompting.

Become a giver.

"The path of a *good woman* is indeed strewn with *flowers*; but they rise behind her steps, not before them."

—JOHN RUSKIN

good works

What is my message of good works?

_ _

_ _

When are the moments that I can
share my message?

_ _

_ _

My Message   My Moment

How can I be a witness to the world as
I live my message?

_ _

_ _

How will living that message help me
to understand my inner worth?

_ _

_ _

My Witness   My Worth

I will have the moral courage to make my actions consistent with my knowledge of right and wrong.

Keeper of

Sincere   Trustworthy   Consistent

Integrity

Devoted   Determined   Full of Honor

Lydia—Keeper of Integrity

The New Testament includes two verses about a woman named Lydia, a seller of purple. We don't know much about Lydia. The scriptures simply tell us that she was a woman who worshipped God.

One Sabbath day Paul and Timothy, two disciples of the Lord, went to preach at a river where people had gathered to pray. Perhaps it was a summer afternoon, and Lydia sat by the riverside and listened to the men teach. As she listened, an important thing happened: the Lord opened her heart, and she found herself paying particular attention to what Paul was talking about. Lydia believed everything Paul taught her and decided to be baptized. From the scriptural account we are led to believe that she was someone that others looked up to, because her whole household followed her example, and they were also baptized.

After she was baptized Lydia offered her home as a place where the disciples could come and stay. Because she was faithful to the Lord we can imagine what her home must have been like, and we know from the scriptures that it became a place where the disciples would gather for refuge and for relief because they felt comfortable there.

Somehow Lydia had left her mark—others were lifted by her example and felt comfortable to be with her because they judged her to be faithful (see Acts 16:14).

I don't really know what it means to be a seller of purple. But I do know that Lydia came from a city that exported purple dye, a highly prized item in this period of history. From her title it seems that Lydia must have been part of this dye industry. Perhaps she was someone who worked in the art of dyeing clothing purple. I like to think that may have been the case, because the dye would have certainly left a mark on her hands, a purple reminder of who she was—a seller of purple.

We can learn much about integrity from Lydia, seller of purple. She was a woman whose heart was open. She knew how important it was to pay attention to what she was taught, and to live that example. Because of her example others were led to believe in the Lord. We also know that her home was a place that was filled with a welcoming spirit, a place where the believers loved to gather.

It is fitting that the value integrity is represented by the color purple, because it will remind us of this story. Perhaps each of us could think of ourselves as a "seller of purple," just like Lydia. What we have to offer is our integrity, and hopefully it will leave a mark on us, and on everyone we meet.

"*Till I die I will not remove mine integrity from me*" (Job 27:5).

Do you leave a mark?

Do you know what a cairn is? It is a carefully stacked pile of rocks used as a trail marker for hikers. Several years ago I was on a hike with a large group of people. As is often the case on hikes, there was a really fast group and then a slower group. Halfway through the hike my group—the slower one—came to a place in the road where the trail split. We didn't know whether we were supposed to go right or left, and the leader of the hike had gone ahead with the fast group. As we gathered together wondering which path we should take, I noticed a cairn that had been placed marking the trail to the left. Immediately I knew it was the path we were supposed to take—our friends had left us a mark.

Consider your own life for a minute.

Are you a confidence keeper? Can your friends trust that their name is safe with you?

When you text or e-mail, is your conversation always appropriate?

Do you do the job right the first time, even if no one is going to check?

Are you consistent? What do you do when people aren't watching? Are you the same person at church that you are at school? Are you the same person with your family that you are with your friends?

There is something remarkable about someone who is true at all times. You never know who might be watching you, even when you can't see them. Learn to never write, text, or share something that you do not want the whole world to know. I love a quote by Richard Bach that says, "Live never to be ashamed if anything you do or say is published around the world."

Live with integrity. Become a seller of purple.

Then you will leave a mark for good on everyone you meet.

What it isn't . . .

Constantly **changing.**

Being **inconsistent** and **undependable.**

Becoming **unsteady.**

Dealing with people **dishonestly.**

What it is . . .

Showing **steadfastness,** honesty, and straightforwardness.

Having **good character.**

Being devoted, **loyal,** and **trustworthy.**

Speaking and acting **fairly** and **sincerely.**

My sister, LauraLee, is a very accomplished tennis player. When she was younger, she had the opportunity to be coached by my grandfather, Harry James, who was the coach of the University of Utah men's tennis team for twenty-five years. He taught my sister a very important lesson on integrity.

What integrity looks like today

One of the hardest things to do in tennis is to make the right call when a ball falls too close to the baseline. Because both the ball and the player are moving so fast, when the ball lands close to the line it is hard to determine which side of the line it was on. Even if one hair of the ball is on the line, it is still considered good.

The person on the opposite side of the court really doesn't have a good view of the ball or the line, and that makes it easy for the other person to cheat. That is why the most important matches have what is called a line judge. Tennis doesn't really need a referee or an umpire; there are so few people on the court. But it does need a line judge to verify that every call is honest.

Line judges are saved for only the most important matches. When players are less experienced they call their own lines. My Grandpa Harry felt that the best tennis players were the ones who were honest. He taught my sister never to call a ball out that had any chance of being in. That way her integrity would never be questioned. So it became LauraLee's habit to play balls that fell as much as twelve inches behind the back line even though they were out. This caused her to become an even better player than she already was.

When my sister was twelve years old, she was invited to compete in the Challenge Cup, an invitational tournament in Florida for the top thirty-six players in the United States in her age bracket. The tournament was held six months after my grandfather died. I don't remember the place she took, but I do remember that she won the sportsmanship award. My mom told my sister, "Grandpa would have been more proud of that sportsmanship award than anything else you could have achieved."

During that event a woman from Florida told my mom, "I am so happy to meet you because I have heard so much about your daughter. We know what a fair competitor she is, and that you never have to wonder about her calls."

Just like Lydia, LauraLee's integrity left a mark—and not just on her, but on everyone she met.

"Integrity is **doing** the **right** thing even if **nobody** **is watching**."

—ANONYMOUS

Accept Integrity

Be true *at all times* in whatsoever thing you are entrusted (see Alma 53:20).

Let your actions be determined by what you know is right.

Understand that integrity requires courage.

You know what is right, just do it.

Be consistent.

Act Upon
Integrity

Try to be the same person at school and at home that you are at church.

Be consistent.

Leave a mark.

Become a seller of purple.

Be trustworthy.

Practice being true in every situation—even when no one is watching.

Keep your commitments.

"*Purity of heart is blooming the same colors in the middle of the wilderness when no one sees you.*"

—VANNA BONTA

integrity

What is my message of integrity?

~~~~~~~~~~~~~~~~~~~~~~~~~~~~

~~~~~~~~~~~~~~~~~~~~~~~~~~~~

When are the moments that I can
share my message?

~~~~~~~~~~~~~~~~~~~~~~~~~~~~

~~~~~~~~~~~~~~~~~~~~~~~~~~~~

My Message   My Moment

How can I be a witness to the world as
I live my message?

~~~~~~~~~~~~~~~~~~~~~~~~~~~~~~~~~~~~~

~~~~~~~~~~~~~~~~~~~~~~~~~~~~~~~~~~~~~

How will living that message help me
to understand my inner worth?

~~~~~~~~~~~~~~~~~~~~~~~~~~~~~~~~~~~~~

~~~~~~~~~~~~~~~~~~~~~~~~~~~~~~~~~~~~~

My Witness   My Worth

I will prepare to enter the temple and remain pure and worthy. My thoughts and actions will be based on high moral standards.

Keeper of

Noble   Pure   Strong

Virtue

Full of Fortitude   Devoted   Spotless

The woman who touched Christ's robe— Keeper of Virtue

The first story that comes to mind when I think of virtue is the story of the woman who touched Christ's robe. Do you remember this story?

There was a woman who had been sick for twelve years. She tried everything she could think of to get better, including visiting a number of doctors. The scriptures tell us she suffered many things and spent all the money she had in her effort to become well, but nothing worked. Even after all she had done she did not get better, and in fact, she grew worse.

Somehow this woman had heard of Jesus, and so she came to the place where He was. A crowd surrounded the Savior as He walked, and she must have realized as He passed her by that He had no time to stop. Still, her faith in His power remained. Perhaps she knew that she was considered unclean, and that meant she could not touch the Savior, but she believed that she could be made whole if she could just get close enough to Him—if she could simply touch His clothes.

As the Savior approached, the woman came up behind Him and touched His garment. Straightway she was healed, and immediately the Savior knew that *virtue* had gone out of Him. If we look at the footnote for *virtue* we see that the Greek translation is "strength." In her hour of need, this woman reached out for the Savior and immediately received virtue, or strength, beyond her own. She was healed.

Jesus immediately started looking through the crowd. He knew the difference between being jostled by the crowd and the touch of faith. He wanted to know who had touched Him. "And he looked round about to see *her* that had done this thing" (Mark 5:32, emphasis added). It is important to notice that He looked round about to see *her*. He knew who had touched Him. In the large crowd of people, the woman might have thought her simple act of faith would go unnoticed. But not by Him.

"When the woman saw that she was not hid" (Luke 8:47), the scriptures tell us she came forward "fearing, trembling, *knowing*" (Mark 5:33, emphasis added). She knew what had happened, and she fell at the Savior's feet and told Him the truth. "She declared unto him before all the people for what cause she had touched him, and how she was healed immediately" (Luke 8:47). And the Savior said unto her, "Daughter, be of good comfort: thy faith hath made thee whole" (Luke 8:48).

To me this story is a powerful example of virtue. In her hour of need this woman turned to the Savior and received strength beyond her own. From this scripture we understand that a woman of virtue is a woman of strength. I believe that the addition of virtue to the Young Women values is essential in the world we live in today. We need more women of strength.

"Who can find a virtuous woman?
for her price is far above rubies"

(PROVERBS 31:10).

How can we learn to be women of strength?

It takes practice.

How do you practice having virtue?

Think of the thirteenth article of faith: "If there is anything virtuous, lovely, or of good report or praiseworthy, we seek after these things." Anything virtuous would be anything that gives you strength. Think of the movies you watch, the books you read, the music you listen to. How about the conversations you have with your friends. Do all of those things make you stronger? More importantly, do they strengthen your testimony of Christ?

If what you are about to do won't strengthen your testimony of Christ, learn to walk away from it. Leave it behind. In the world we live in today, you can't afford to waste time on anything that will not make you stronger.

In Proverbs 31 we read some of the characteristics of a virtuous woman. She is a woman who can be trusted, a woman who chooses good over evil. She is a hard worker, one who brings honor to her home. A virtuous woman stretches out her hand to the poor and remembers those who are needy. Her light shines through the darkness. She knows how to dress, and her clothing is fit for the daughter of a king. A virtuous woman is wise beyond her years and kind to all she meets.

She is a woman who is strong, because she has practiced standing up for what is most important.

Her strength comes from the Lord.

What it isn't . . .

Bringing **dishonor**
upon yourself.

Showing **weakness** when
faced with temptation.

Failing to avoid **evil.**

Living immorally.

What it is . . .

Having **high** moral **standards.**

Daring to live **righteously.**

Earning **respect.**

Being **honorable** and strong.

It was a two-mile trek up to Silver Lake, just perfect for a hike at girl's camp.

What virtue looks like today

The Young Women group climbed the wooded trail, passing through aspen trees and pausing for a couple of rest stops along the way. The hike was strenuous, and after a while Samantha, one of the young Beehives, became worried that she wouldn't be able to make it the rest of the way.

Her leaders encouraged her as they climbed, lightening her load and stopping for breaks, and for a time one of the leaders carried her piggyback as they followed the path. But as they neared the top of the mountain the steepness of the trail forced everyone to stop for a rest, and the leader who had been carrying Sam set her down, knowing she wouldn't be able to carry her up the rocky ridge.

Even with the short rest, Samantha worried that she wouldn't make it; she was too worn out for the final push to the top. The leaders gathered around Sam offering words of encouragement, "You can do it; you're going to make it." As they talked, Samantha's fourteen-year-old sister, Kacey, came up beside them, and without pausing to rest, lifted Samantha onto her back. Then she began climbing up the steepest and most treacherous part of the hike, clinging to each rock for added strength as she carried her sister up the hill.

Watching Kacey climb, the leaders were impressed with her strength and stamina, especially because it came at the end of the hike, but they were even more impressed with her attitude—she knew she could do it, and she was willing to sacrifice to make sure her sister made it to the top. She found a source of inner strength—strength enough to lift another until she could walk again on her own.

Each of us will have opportunities to lift someone. The Lord encourages us to "succor the weak, lift up the hands which hang down, and strengthen the feeble knees" (D&C 81:5). As we go through life, we will meet people who are looking for someone they can lean on for strength. Someone might find strength in the way they see you dress, and choose to be more modest because of your example. Some may find strength from the words you speak, or the way you treat other people. Many will rely on your strength as you stand up for what you believe. Your testimony of the Savior will become a strength to those who surround you, and many will lean on your testimony until theirs become just as strong. Your strength will lead others to know the Lord.

When you are virtuous you have an inner strength that makes you strong—strong enough to lift another until they find the strength to stand on their own.

"Give me a **young woman** who is **virtuous** . . . and I will **give** you a young woman who will perform **miracles** for the Lord **now** and throughout **eternity.**"

—EZRA TAFT BENSON
("TO THE YOUNG WOMEN OF THE CHURCH,"
ENSIGN, NOVEMBER 1986, 81)

Accept Virtue

A woman of virtue is a woman of strength.

Let your thoughts and actions be determined by the strength
of your high moral standards.

Find strength by making temple visits a regular
part of your life.

In times of trouble, remember: you can turn to the
Lord for strength.

Rely on your inner strength.

Live Strong.

Act Upon Virtue

The Lord needs young women who are pure and worthy.

Let people know that you seek after things that are virtuous, praiseworthy, and of good report.

If it won't strengthen your testimony of Christ, walk away from it.

Let others lean on you until they find strength to stand alone.

Find strength in the Lord.

Visit the temple regularly.

Be strong.

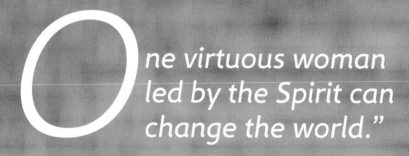

One virtuous woman led by the Spirit can change the world."

—ELAINE S. DALTON

virtue

What is my message of virtue?

. . . .

. . . .

When are the moments that I can share my message?

. . . .

. . . .

My Message   My Moment

How can I be a witness to the world
as I live my message?

· ·

· ·

How will living that message help me
to understand my inner worth?

· ·

· ·

My Witness   My Worth

Hopefully you are well on your way to discovering your message to the world.

Now you have to decide how you will live that message. Finding moments in your life to share that message will not only increase your worth, but it will also strengthen your testimony. It is important to remember that you are not alone! As you live these eight values you "join with thousands of other young women who are striving to come unto Christ and stand as a witness" (Young Women Personal Progress, 1).

Your message to the world

What does it mean to stand as a witness? I am reminded of the scripture found in 1 Peter 3:15: "Be ready always to give an answer to every man that asketh you a reason of the hope that is in you." We never know when someone might be watching or learning from our example. We must be ready always. That is why it is so important to stand as a witness at *all times, and in all things, and in all places.*

The summer before my senior year, my dad was called as a mission president to the California Ventura Mission. When we got to Ventura we didn't have any friends, so my brothers and sisters and I all hung out together. Often we would go on outings with my parents. Right away we discovered that my dad had a new habit that would take some getting used to. Everywhere we went he would ask whomever we happened to meet three simple questions: Have you ever heard of the LDS Church? Do you know anybody who is a Mormon? And, Would you like to know more?

I will be honest: sometimes it could be pretty embarrassing. So all of us kids made it a point to escape before the moment when my dad would ask the questions. If we were at a grocery store checkout line we would take the keys and tell my dad we would see him in the car just as he got ready to pop the question. If we were in a restaurant we would all make an emergency trip to the bathroom while he talked to the waiter. You get the idea.

I'll never forget what happened one evening as we pull into the drive-thru at Taco Bell. We drove a thirteen-seater van. (It was the easiest way to transport the most missionaries.) Because we had six kids, our family had a drive-thru rule: each child would make their way to the driver's side window to order and then move to the back of the car—that way my dad didn't have to remember everybody's order.

As was the custom, we each ordered and then moved to the very back two rows of the van—we knew the three questions were coming! Sure enough, as my dad paid he asked the young girl standing at the window, "Have you ever heard of the LDS Church?" She replied that she knew a little, but not very much. Then he asked her, "Do you know anybody who is a

Mormon?" She replied, "I know just one, Emily Oswald." That was my name! I leaned over the seat to look in the window of the Taco Bell, but I didn't recognize the girl. She must have gone to my new high school, but I had never formally met her.

As we drove home I wondered where she had seen me, and more importantly, what I had been doing. I hoped I had been doing something good. If I was the only representative of the Church that she had ever seen, I hope I was a good one. I hope my actions were a witness of my testimony of Jesus Christ. I hope I was living up to my responsibilities as a keeper.

That moment changed my life forever. It was the first time I really understood how crucial it is to "stand as a witness of God at all times and in all things, and in all places as we strive to live the Young Women values."

We never know who is watching.

Have **faith** that you are a daughter
of Heavenly Father who loves you.

Determine which of your **divine gifts**
will allow you to be a champion for Christ.

Realize that you have been sent to Earth
with a **divine mission** that is yours to achieve.

Let your **knowledge** come from the
good parts of life that surround you.

Choose to set high standards and defend them.

Become a great woman by **doing good.**
Always be on the Lord's errand.

Leave your mark. Be **true** in every situation—
even when no one is watching.

Let your strength come from
having **high moral standards**.

Never forget that you have come to the Earth at this particular time for a sacred and glorious purpose. You have a noble calling to use your strength and influence for good (see Young Women Personal Progress). This is your moment. Share your message. You have so much to offer.

Heavenly Father knows who you are, but even more importantly, He knows who you can become. He sent His Son to guide you, promising that "the Lord is thy keeper" (Psalm 121:5). Jesus Christ is the greatest keeper of all—He will protect you, guard you, and look after you because you are important, precious, and valuable. He loves you and He has miracles in store for you.

Look to Him.

Stand as His witness.

Become a keeper
of what matters most.

About the Author

Emily Freeman's writing reflects a deep love of the scriptures and a strong desire to share their application in modern-day life. She is the author of several books, including *The Promise of Enough: Seven Principles of True Abundance* and *21 Days Closer to Christ*. Emily and her husband, Greg, are the parents of four children and live in Lehi, Utah.

Visit Emily's website at www.emilyfreeman.com. You can also visit *Keepers of What Matters Most* on facebook.com

Acknowledgments

Many thanks to Carolyn and Abbie-Kate Apsley, Lisa and Kelsee Coombs, Lisa and Melissa Fraughton, Shelly and Hadlee Labrum, Donna and Nicole Lyman, Melissa and Maggie Matheny, Tasha and Samantha Murphy, Josephine and Victoria North, Hilary and Mckenzie Weeks, Sara Allen, Christine Beardall, Kris Belcher, Angela Bennett, Lisa Blanck, Megan Freeman, Sharee Hills, Leslie Oswald, Mickie Neslen, Rachel Pickney, Deborah Savage, and many others for their advice and encouragement.

Heartfelt appreciation to Jana Erickson whose vision, enthusiasm, and direction made this book what it is. Her love of the Young Women program is evident, and can be felt throughout the pages of this book.

I am indebted to a wonderful team at Deseret Book, whose tremendous talent continues to surpass all my expectations. Thank you for your creativity and attention to detail. Special thanks to Leslie Stitt, Shauna Gibby, Richard Erickson, Tonya Facemyer, and Sheryl Dickert Smith.

And last, to a new generation of young women, including my daughter Megan, and soon Grace, who are learning to live and love these values. Thank you for living what you believe. It matters. Really, it does.

Photo credits

Emily Freeman: page vi.
Shutterstock: flowers and balloons throughout the book, pages 38, 128, 136.
Shutterstock: flowers on cover.
Jupiter Images Unlimited: pages 16–17, 22, 30–31, 41, 48–49, 56, 64–65, 72, 80–81, 88, 96–97, 104, 112–13, 120, 144–45, 148.